The Lawyer's Advisor

Maxims and Precepts for Lawyers, Students and Clients

by
James Moss

ICS BOOKS, Inc.
Merrillville, IN

The Lawyer's Advisor

10 9 8 7 6 5 4 3 2 1

All inquiries should be addressed to ICS Books, Inc., 1370 E. 86th Place, Merrillville, IN 46410

Published by:
ICS BOOKS, Inc.
1370 E. 86th Place
Merrillville, IN 46410
800-541-7323

Printed in the U.S.A.

Library of Congress Cataloging-in-Publication Data

Moss, James.
The lawyer's advisor : maxims and precepts for lawyer's and clients
/ by James Moss.
p. cm . -- (Advisor series ; v. 1)
ISBN 1-57034-050-1
1. Law--United States -- Quotations, maxims, etc. I. Title.
II. Series.
KF159. M67 1996
349.73 -- dc20
[347.3] 96-33985
CIP

Table of Contents

Acknowledgments

I would like to acknowledge my parents Jim and Loretta Moss for giving me common sense, concern and passion. My brother and sister for showing me how to put them in use and The Boy Scouts of America for building upon the foundation provided by my parents. Finally, I would like to acknowledge the many people in the world who have called my office with questions that contributed to this book.

I would also like to acknowledge common sense. It seems to be lacking in most of today's world. Following common sense in the lost attribute's department is courtesy and concern for another person rather than the all mighty dollar. If these three traits were found in more people, I would be out of a job.

Introduction

I decided one year to advertise in the yellow pages as a consumer lawyer. What twist of fate created this desire I do not understand, however, the phone calls I received were outrageous. Many seemed to be people who if they stepped back and looked at their situation would gently chuckle over their predicament. Some were truly horrific stories of the elderly being ripped off or a consumer being conned. All of the calls involved greed or a lack of the obvious.

Many times tit was quite easy to solve the case if an injury was involved. Many people said they wanted someone to say "I'm sorry." Unless it was an attempt to rip off the caller, most issues were handled over the phone by stepping back and examining the problem. I never made enough money from the phone calls to pay for the yellow page ad, however, I was constantly amazed by the calls.

DISCLAIMER

All legal advice by its nature is subject to review by your local attorney. Laws vary by state, county and city. Your fact situation and the laws of your state may alter any advice in this book. I suggest you consult an attorney before implementing any advice contained herein.

When You Will Need a Lawyer

You may need a lawyer to review a contract if you do not like the person with whom you are dealing.

You may need a lawyer to review a contract if the total amount of consideration is more than the credit limit on your credit card.

You may need a lawyer to review a contract if there is an interest rate on the document.

You may need a lawyer to review a contract if there is a "Notice" provision on the document.

You may need a lawyer to review a contract if the salesperson has visited your house to make the sale.

You may need a lawyer to review a contract if you feel as if you do not have any choice in signing the contract.

You may need a lawyer to review a contract if there is a deadline before which you have to sign the contract.

You may need a lawyer to review a contract if it requires a witness to verify your signature.

You may need a lawyer to review a contract if it says "Please read."

You may need a lawyer if someone is reading you your rights.

You may need a lawyer if you have handcuffs on and you are not in your bedroom.

You may need a lawyer if your monthly bills total more money than you make in a month.

You may need a lawyer if you are in a hospital and you do not know why or how you got there.

You may need a lawyer if you had an accident and you spent more than 12 hours in the hospital.

You may need a lawyer to review a contract if there are a series of dates before which you must accomplish something or pay a specified amount.

You may need a lawyer to review a contract if it lists the rights you are giving up.

The Law

Laws vary from state to state.

The laws of the United States are based on the common law of England.

The laws of Louisiana are based on the laws of France.

Most laws have a reason. Understand the reason, and you will understand the law. Law school does not necessarily teach you the reason; experience does.

Laws can be established two ways: by legislative decree or by order of a court.

Laws are enforced by punishment, either monetary damages or incarceration.

Petty laws breed great crimes.
—Ouida

If you like laws and sausages, you should never watch either one being made.
—Otto von Bismarck

The best way to get a bad law repealed is to enforce it strictly.
—Abraham Lincoln

The most important office ... that of private citizen.
—Louis D. Brandeis

No man was ever endowed with a right without being at the same time saddled with a responsibility.
—Gerald W. Johnson

Many a person seems to think it is not enough for the government to guarantee him the pursuit of happiness. He insists it also run interference for him.
—Anonymous

I disapprove of what you say, but will defend to the death your right to say it.
—Voltaire

I have always been among those who believed that the greatest freedom of speech was the greatest safety, because if a man is a fool the best thing to do is to encourage him to advertise the fact by speaking.
—Woodrow Wilson

Most laws are made to keep the rich secure and the poor in line. If you question this, walk through a courthouse.

The remaining laws are meant to tax the rich and the poor.

A tort is the name of a lawsuit where one person has injured another person or his property. Torts usually follow automobile accidents, explosions, or other accidents where people or property are injured.

Contracts are promises. A breach-of-contract lawsuit results when someone breaks a promise.

Some laws are created by the legislature. Age discrimination and civil rights violations are examples of these.

Age discrimination requires that the person who is discriminated against be over the age of 40.

Settling Possible and Probable Lawsuits

When confronted with a legal problem, compare the cost of the lawyer to the cost of avoiding or resolving the problem. Most of the time, it is cheaper to turn down the stereo.

Always determine your actual loss in addition to the potential gains when evaluating a lawsuit.

Your losses can include costs, attorney fees, claims the other side may have against you, and your time.

Determine your loss both if you do sue and if you do not sue.

Don't be too proud to settle a lawsuit.

Ninety-eight percent of all lawsuits are settled before trial.

Any settlement offer made to your lawyer must be communicated to you.

The easiest way to stay out of a lawsuit is to say "I'm sorry."

Remember what your mother taught you when you were growing up. Treat people the way you want to be treated and you should never see the inside of a courtroom, unless you take a tour.

Arbitration is the process where a neutral party makes a quick decision rather than have the parties slog out a dispute in court.

Mediation is where a neutral party attempts to resolve a problem by getting the parties closer together.

One man's word is no man's word; we should quietly hear both sides.
—Johann Wolfgang von Goethe

In a dispute, break down the problem into little parts and work at solving each little one. If a small problem cannot be resolved, move on and come back to it later.

For the most part, avoid courtrooms and trials at all costs.

Lawsuits

Courts only deal with money. Do not use the courts to resolve emotional issues.

A subpoena is a legal document requiring your attendance at court or a lawyer's office. When you receive a subpoena, call the lawyer named on it to find out what is going on — and if you need your own lawyer.

If you feel you do have grounds for a lawsuit, make sure you know the time limit in which you must file your lawsuit.

The time limit in which to file your lawsuit is called the statute of limitations. A statute of limitation can be as short as 30 days.

It's not worth suing if the defendant does not have any money.

Principles do not pay bills, do not send you on a vacation, and do not provide great victories. Make sure continuing a lawsuit based on principles is worth the emotional victory.

Do not start your lawsuit until you or your lawyer has all the facts. Do not file your lawsuit too early.

Even friends, upon receiving subpoenas to testify at a trial, can be uncomfortable or upset.

Make sure you understand all facets of the lawsuit, and base your expectations realistically.

In every courtroom there is one winning attorney and one losing attorney.

Most people sue because of emotions, not money.

TV law is entertainment. Do not confuse entertainment with your case.

O.J. Simpson's trial has as much relationship to a normal criminal trial as your chances of flying the space shuttle.

You cannot sue someone for an injury if you understood and assumed the risk of the injury.

You cannot recover from someone if you are the major cause of your injuries.

Do not threaten to sue unless you have the means to do so and intend to do so.

American society believes money solves all problems. Broken arms, broken promises, and broken hearts are all dealt with the same way: with money.

Evidence is used to prove a case at trial. A statement of a witness is evidence.

You will probably only recover your actual loss, not your potential gain.

The down-side of any lawsuit is the time you must spend on it.

Lawyers and Dealing with Them

Lawyers are not judges.

Most judges are lawyers.

If your judge is not a lawyer, find yourself a lawyer.

Lawyers are people created by the goals, desires, and greed of their clients.

Second opinions are a good idea when dealing with lawyers — and a lot of other people.

Many lawyers provide free or cheap initial consultations. Those who advertise free consultations are usually personal injury attorneys.

Personal injury attorneys represent people injured in automobile accidents, employment injuries and so forth.

Defense attorneys represent those accused of injuring someone or those accused of a crime.

Find an attorney who specializes in your problem.

Attorneys who specialize in a particular area may charge more, but they usually work faster, understand your problem quicker, and can do the job cheaper than someone who does not specialize in your problem.

Lawyers live and die by paper. Always take all your paperwork when you go to meet your attorney.

Always insist that your attorney send you copies of all documents he generates or receives in your case.

If you have a problem, find a lawyer, not a law firm.

If you own a large corporation, look for a lawyer with a firm.

Your legal bills should always tell you what was done and how long it took. Costs and expenses should be not hidden in the overall charge.

Lawyers only deal in money. They cannot resolve a problem, except by using money. They cannot repair or replace; they can only get the dollar's value of the repair or replacement.

Everyone makes mistakes. Remember that before you go to a lawyer and after you start dealing with one.

Most sole practitioners make less than $40,000.00 per year in the practice of law.

Do not use a lawyer's name as a threat or a reference unless you know him and have worked with him in the past.

Do not think that, just because you hired a lawyer the first time, you do not need him the second time. The laws change every day.

A courtroom is the place where lawyers compete, using your problem as the goal to resolve.

A lawyer, doctor, or other professional cannot contract away malpractice.

Lawyers are the catalysts for what goes around comes around.
—Buck Tilton

If you have any doubts as to whether or not you need a lawyer to assist you, you need a lawyer.

There are three basic forms of fee agreements with attorneys: fixed fees, time-based fees, and contingency fee agreements.

A fixed fee agreement is specific work for a set price.

A time-based fee agreement is based on the amount of time it takes to do the work at an hourly or daily rate.

A contingency fee agreement pays the lawyer when the lawyer recovers money for the client.

Contingent fee agreements are used to collect bad debts and for personal injury actions.

No one practicing law can make a promise on the outcome except that it will take longer than expected.

Never use an attorney who treats his staff badly. The attorney will treat you the same way.

Always tell your lawyer the truth.

Always tell your lawyer everything.

Most lawyers love homemade cookies.

When comparing hourly rates, remember that you get what you pay for.

When negotiating your bill, ask to be billed in the smallest time increments— in six-minute increments rather than 15-minute increments.

Pay your lawyer on time; a lawyer is not a bank.

Whenever you leave a message for your lawyer, leave your name and phone number. You will be charged for the time it takes to look up your phone number.

You will be called back sooner if you leave your name and phone number. The easiest phone calls are called back first.

Always be pleasant when leaving a message for your lawyer. The receptionist is not your lawyer and is not responsible for his actions.

Always be polite when leaving messages for your lawyer.

Never fire your lawyer in anger.

Never get mad at your lawyer when he gives you bad news. He is just doing his job.

No work starts until your lawyer has been paid.

The faster you pay your legal bill, the faster your case proceeds.

Sometimes it is cheaper to hire a local attorney to coordinate your-out-of state legal bills.

Most lawyers work long hours. This does not mean you should wait till 7:00 P.M. to call.

The majority of lawyers are poor golfers. They do not have time.

If you meet a lawyer on the golf course, his skill at golf will usually be the inverse of his legal skills.

When scheduling an appointment with an attorney, ask what documents to bring with you to the appointment.

Unless it is for business or for making a will, you are seeing an attorney because you screwed up.

Do not pay for your attorney's time if you are not willing to listen.

Do not pay for your attorney's time if you are not willing to learn.

Do not pay for your attorney's time if you are not willing to change.

Your lawyer is not your therapist. Make sure you understand that.

Do not pay an attorney to be your therapist. If he insists, find another lawyer.

Pay your lawyer to solve your problems, not to listen to why they occurred.

Go prepared to your lawyer's office or do not go at all.

Ask your lawyer what you should bring to each meeting, then bring everything.

If you have a lot of documents, sometimes it is easier to have your lawyer visit you.

If you are going to hire a lawyer, make sure the fight is worth your time.

A lawyer is a person legally appointed by another to act as his or her agent in the transaction of business, specifically one qualified and licensed to act for plaintiffs and defendants in legal proceedings.
—The American Heritage® Dictionary of the English Language, Third Edition copyright © 1992 by Houghton Mifflin Company

A lawyer is one whose profession is to give legal advice and assistance to clients and represent them in court or in other legal matters.
—The American Heritage® Dictionary of the English Language, Third Edition copyright © 1992 by Houghton Mifflin Company

Lawyers know life practically.
—Samuel Johnson (1709–84)

If there were no bad people, there would be no good lawyers.
—Charles Dickens (1812–70)

He who represents himself has a fool for a client.

No client walks into a lawyer's office happy or with good news.

Clients only see a lawyer when they have a problem.

Lawyers are products of their clients' needs and desires. Attorneys' responses to a problem are based on the needs or wants of clients. The lawyer works to win for the client, not lose.

A lawyer is an advisor, not a boss. Your lawyer is not being paid to judge you; he is being paid to advocate for you, to win for you.

If you are not going to tell your lawyer everything, truthfully, do not waste your money or his time.

Do not pay for your attorney's time if you are not willing to change or accept the consequences of not changing.

Never go to a lawyer's office without something to write on and with. Why go if you are not going to safeguard and remember what you learned?

Lawyers enjoy a little mystery, you know. Why, if everybody came forward and told the truth, the whole truth, and nothing but the truth straight out, we should all retire to the workhouse.
—Dorothy L. Sayers (1893–1957)

A lawyer is not always paid for what he is doing for you, but for the time when he cannot work for someone else because of you.

A lawyer is paid for the time he waits for you to get off the phone or to finish your other meeting.

Lawyers charge more to review work you have done than for them to do it right the first time.

Lawyers hear promises every day. Promising future work for a present answer fools no one.

You cannot save money by telling your lawyer when and when not to charge you in preparing for a case; you can only lose the case.

If you like your days off, allow your lawyer to enjoy his days off also.

Most lawyers like to be called at home because they will triple their bill for that phone call at home. Some lawyers just charge a flat $100.00 for phone calls at home.

No one ever walks into a lawyer's office with a big smile on his face and exclaims, "Guess what happened to me today!"

Lawyers make more money from people making mistakes than from people doing things right the first time.

Most lawyers are a little cynical, very inquisitive, and extremely intense. What they are not born with, law school beats into them.

If the truth, the whole truth, and nothing but the truth were the absolute rule of law and life, there would be no need for lawyers.

No one practicing law can make a promise on any lawsuit except that it will cost more than expected.

Always keep track of the expenses in your case. Inflated expenses are an easy way to overpay a lawyer.

The best defense is a good offense. You will pay your lawyer to study and think about what the other side is going to do.

Lawyers are the first line of defense in individual freedoms.

Judges and Courts

Most judges are lawyers, but not all.

If you are in front of a judge who is not a lawyer, make sure you have a lawyer with you.

No matter what the judge says, the court clerks run the courthouse.

Leave cameras and tape recorders at home. It will be too dark to take a picture, and someone else has the job of recording the proceedings.

Always take a pad and pen to court. The judge will always tell you something important. If nothing else, the judge will tell you when to come back.

For every hour you spend in court, it requires a minimum of three hours to get you ready and several more hours to get the attorney and the paperwork ready.

The penalty for laughing in a courtroom is six months in jail; if it were not for this penalty, the jury would never hear the evidence.
—H.L. Mencken

A courtroom is "...a place where they dispense with justice."
—Arthur Train

A court is a place where what was confused before becomes more unscttled than ever.
—Henry Waldorf Francis

Most trials are not to determine who is right, but to find out who is the least wrong.

Remember when voting for President of the United States, his term may only last four or eight years. The judges appointed by the President serve for life.

If a lawyer tells you he can fix the case, the judge, or the prosecutor, run. You are dealing with a crook and probably a liar.

Most lawyers are friends with judges; friendship is not illegal.

All states have a small claims court where lawyers are not allowed. You can argue small disputes in small claims court for little cost and time.

If you cannot resolve the problem any other way, take it to small claims court.

If the amount in question is too large for small claims court, hire a lawyer.

Most people spend the most time in courthouses waiting. Be prepared to do the same when you go to the courthouse.

Do not take your children into the courthouse and never into the courtroom. Courtrooms are quieter than libraries, and there is nothing to do but sit and wait.

If you are scheduled for a hearing or trial at 9:00 A.M., be there at 9:00 A.M. Even though the judge may not get to your case until 9:30, the judge will declare you absent at 9:15.

Judges are human. They understand the problem.

It is better to tell the judge you slept through your hearing than to make up a more believable story that is false.

If you cannot make it to court because your car broke down, bring a towing receipt, bus token, cab receipt, or the friend who gave you the ride when you do get to court.

Courts make people nervous, including lawyers. Speak slowly and clearly.

Treat the court clerk with respect. If you don't, the judge will teach you respect.

Leave money, knives, guns, drugs, and chains at home. Most courthouses have metal detectors.

There is no such thing as justice—in or out of court.
—Clarence Darrow

Consumer Law and Sense

Monopolies are companies that have the exclusive right to do a specific business in a certain area. Most telephone, gas, electric, and other public service companies are monopolies.

Monopolies are hard to fight and always take a lot of time. Before you fight the monopoly, understand the monopoly.

Your credit report is valuable; check it yearly.

When you lease, you are paying someone to borrow something. When you purchase something on credit, you own it; you are just paying for it over time.

Everything comes with a warranty. Usually even when it says it does not, it still does.

One of the reasons why people selling things on the phone use the phone, is that they do not want you to recognize their faces.

If your health club requires you to sign a contract for a period of time, make sure you really want to exercise. No matter what, you will owe the money or the payments even if you do not work-out or you move.

If someone wants money or a deposit before you can win your prize or get your money, it's a ripoff.

The easiest way to be ripped off is to buy an item when it is available only for a limited time at the "sale" price.

The FTC (Federal Trade Commission) maintains brochures on hundreds of consumer services and cons.

You can call the FTC to find out the reasonable cost of funeral services and products.

When you purchase items at a store, you may or may not be able to take them back. Check before you make the purchase if you are not sure about the policy or the product.

If you purchase something in your home for more than $25.00, you have three days to cancel your purchase, with some exceptions.

To cancel a contract within a three-day period, you must sign and date one copy of the cancellation form or write a letter and mail it to the seller. The envelope must be post-marked before the cancellation period ends.

You do not have to give a reason for canceling; you can just change your mind.

Giving a reason to a salesperson for not wanting to buy something just gives him another opportunity to sell to you. Just say no.

Remember when you sign an "automatic debit" form, you are giving someone the right to enter your checking account and with-draw money every month. Stopping automatic debit plans is usually difficult.

"No fee" means you do not have to pay any money — at all. If that changes sometime during the transaction, get out immediately.

If you think you look good and want to be paid big bucks for your looks, you are a prime target for modeling agency scams. Once you are selected to be a model, you are presented with a contract requiring you to pay hundreds of dollars for "extras."

If you have not heard of the charity, do not give them any money.

Give money to charities that you know and understand, not just based on the pictures of the people they supposedly help.

If you do not recognize the charity as being from your community, do not give them any money. Why send money to help people in another community when there is probably someone in yours that needs your help.

If you want to send money to another community or state to help someone, do so through a nationally recognized organization like the American Red Cross.

You should check out a charity's expenses before contributing money. Those that spend more money on themselves than the people they are supposed to help may not be where you want your money to go.

Just because your warranty has expired does not mean the problem will not be fixed. If you complained about a problem before the warranty ended and the problem was not fixed, the problem should be fixed for free even if the warranty period has ended.

If you do not have a warranty in writing, you probably do not have much of a warranty.

If you order something through the mail or over the phone, make sure you know how long it will take for delivery. If the product has not arrived by the stated time, you can cancel the sale without penalty.

If you go to a grocery store to buy an item advertised at a special price, you can get a rain check, unless the ad stated, "Quantities are limited."

Just because the envelope says "National," "Service," or sounds like a federal government agency does not mean it is. Federal envelopes are easy to spot and easily identified.

Envelopes designed to look like or mimic those of the federal government probably contain a ripoff or are sent by collection agencies.

Most publications about taxes you buy in the supermarket are identical to the ones you can get from the IRS for free.

When buying something by mail, if the company does not state when your order will be shipped, it must be shipped in 30 days.

If you are buying by mail and applying for credit, the company has 50 days to ship your order.

Art is to look at, not to invest in over the phone.

If an artist is starving, he will probably go get a job at a fast food restaurant.

If you have never heard of the "strategic metal" being sold to you over the phone, do not buy it.

Once you make one "scam" investment, you will get offers for several more. "Suckers lists" contain the names and phone numbers of people who have previously fallen prey. They are circulated around the industry or just around the room.

You can tell a collection agency not to contact you at work.

Once you give the collection agency your attorney's name and phone number, they are not allowed to contact you again. Make sure the attorney knows he is working for you.

Collection agencies are not allowed to call at odd hours or to harass or threaten you.

There are few federal standards for "green" or environmental standards. Be wary of products that advertise their environmental friendliness but do not have the ability to stand behind their claims.

A negative option plan describes a program where you have to notify the company that you do not want a product that is about to be sent.

Signing up for a book, video, CD, or other plan is another type of contract, a negative option plan. If you do not complete the contract by purchasing the required number of products, it can affect your credit rating.

Some dance studios have sold dance lesson contracts that last longer than the buyer will live.

Find the correct name and address for the Federal Trade Commission, your state attorney general's consumer fraud unit, your city attorney's consumer fraud unit, the Better Business Bureau, and any local consumer protection agencies. When writing a complaint letter, note at the bottom of the letter that you have sent copies to them — and *send them copies.*

The most powerful part of a complaint letter is the section denoting who receives copies.

If you indicate on the bottom of your letter that you have sent a copy of the letter to someone, you'd better send them a copy of the letter.

When you send copies of your complaint letter to third parties, make sure your letter is clear enough and recites enough of the facts for the third parties to understand what is happening.

When writing a complaint letter, identify the item you are complaining about as well as how, why, and what went wrong.

When writing a complaint letter, tell them what you want. Complaining without asking for a solution requires that the seller try to read your mind.

Most reputable manufacturers and retailers want to know about a problem. They also want satisfied customers.

No one likes to deal with crazy people over a $40.00 product. Be polite, specific, and patient when dealing with a problem.

Treat a retailer or manufacturer with respect, be honest, and explain what happened and what you want. If that does not work, get out your pen/computer and write to everyone.

Everyone has a boss. If you are not getting what you want, politely ask to move up one level.

Just because someone's boss is not in does not mean you cannot talk to him. Get his name and address and write a letter, letting him know his subordinate would not let you talk to him. Send a copy to the subordinate.

If you cannot get the boss's name, the secretary of state of the state in which the company is doing business has the president's name. Write to the president of the company.

The squeaky wheel gets the oil.

A squeak is a constant and persistent noise; it is not screaming and yelling.

Some magazines stand by their advertisers. Even those that do not stand by their advertisers do not want to hear that you are dissatisfied with the magazine because they allow fraudulent companies to place ads with them.

If you are contacted out of the blue by a government-sounding group claiming to be trying to help you because you were taken by a telemarketer, be wary. How did they find out about you? It is probably just another telemarketing scam.

"Bait and switch" involves first advertising an item at a very low price. Then, when a customer attempts to buy the product he is encouraged to switch to a similar, more expensive product with the explanation that the original product is already sold out.

Send a copy of your complaint letter to the magazine in which you found the manufacturer's ad.

Be wary of product endorsements from magazines that contain a large number of them. Normally, they are nothing more than the manufacturer's press release.

Cellular phones are free because the contract you are signing pays for the phone. Understand what you are signing when you sign the contract. It may be cheaper to buy the phone.

Cellular phone contracts are contracts. If you do not pay the minimum each month, they will sue you for the money or turn your account over to a collection agency.

With a free special card from the Social Security Administration, you can check your social security account. You should check your account regularly.

Mail the card requesting your social security account information in an envelope. Writing your social security number on a post card broadcasts it to the world. Safeguard your privacy.

Protect your social security number; it is the key to your credit and your privacy.

If your social security number is on your driver's license, someone can check your driving record and get your social security number.

Only the IRS and people who must report to the IRS have the right to know your social security number.

"Bank" is a four-letter word.

A banker is a fellow who lends you his umbrella when the sun is shining, but wants it back the minute it begins to rain.
—Mark Twain, American Writer (1835-1910)

The easiest way to collect a debt is to not allow it to go bad in the beginning.

You cannot yell "fire" in a crowd.

It is better to yell "fire" than "help" when you are in trouble. Help is someone else's problem. Fire affects everyone.

It is easier and less embarrassing to balance your checkbook than to bounce checks. Computer programs make balancing a snap.

No one can check on your credit history without your permission.

It is easy to check someone's driving and criminal record.

If you are robbed or assaulted, remember what was said and what the person looked like.

If you hire someone to work in your home to babysit or clean on a regular or full time basis, you must pay social security taxes for that person. Failure to do so could keep you off the U.S. Supreme Court.

You do not have to pay for merchandise you do not order that comes to your home through the mail.

The Freedom of Information Act (FOIA) gives you the right to find out what a federal agency is keeping on file about you.

If no file exists, a file will be started on you if you write and request FOIA information.

A good deal will always be there tomorrow.

Whenever you are sending documents to back up a complaint or appeal, send copies. Make one set of copies to send and one set to work with. Store originals in a safe place.

When placing your money in a bank or interest-bearing investment, make sure you know the difference between simple and compound interest.

The interest rate advertised is not the interest you will get if you are investing for a period of less than a year.

The ownership of a safe-deposit box is a matter of public record. Do not expect to hide things from the IRS or anyone else in a safe-deposit box.

A smile is the easiest way to mask true feelings.

Asking questions is not impolite or improper; however, we have developed that idea. When in doubt, ask questions.

Burglars like games, not work. Hiding valuables is a game; placing valuables in the attic which requires work to get to is usually safer. Hide your valuables where they are difficult to get to, not just deceptive.

The Privacy Rights Clearinghouse can provide you with more information on protecting your privacy and ultimately your money. Contact them at 619-298-3396.

Electronic Mail, or E-mail, is not private. Anyone along the route can read your E-mail message.

You can contact the Medical Information Bureau at 617-426-3660 to check on the health information they have about you.

Most states, for a nominal fee and proper information, will allow you to check someone's driving record.

With a release, you can usually check someone's criminal record. If your employees are working with children or the elderly, it is worth the time and money to check.

For a nominal fee and a release, someone will check a prospective employee's credit report or worker's compensation history.

Always communicate with your creditors. When you quit communicating with them, they will find a collection agency or lawyer to communicate for them.

Be willing to pay more for service. The small increase in fees will pay enormously when you need to deal with a human rather than a computer.

Make sure you understand the terms on the back of bills of lading and receipts. They will control returns, rejections, insurance, and payments.

If you think you have been defrauded in a sale, contact the National Fraud Information Center Consumer Assistance line at 800-876-7060.

When you write a complaint letter, send copies to any and all agencies that control or supervise the business as well as the Better Business Bureau and the Chamber of Commerce.

Take ten minutes and contact the Better Business Bureau before dealing with a new company.

Even if there is no interest rate stipulated, the law of the state will always supply an interest rate for any money owed.

Each state has a maximum rate of interest that someone charging interest cannot exceed.

Even caskets are sold by salespersons. Be wary whenever anyone attempts to provide anything in exchange for your money.

When you purchase items at a store, you may or may not be able to take them back. Check before you purchase.

If the product has not arrived by the stated time, you can cancel the sale without penalty.

Moving from one state to another should trigger several different changes in your life.

When you move from one state to another state, you will have to change your driver's license within 30 days.

When you move from one state to another, you will have to change your license plates within 30 days.

If you are moving, take your money, jewelry, collections, and other valuables with you.

Before you move, photograph your valuables and large pieces of furniture to prove value if they are lost or damaged.

Make sure your homeowner's insurance covers your property during a move.

Always follow up most communications in writing to make sure both parties understand what was said and expected by each party.

If you get a letter as a follow-up to a phone conversation that is not correct, immediately call and write a follow-up letter making corrections.

If you stop payment by phone on a check with your bank, you usually have 24 hours to get a written notice to the bank.

When moving to a new state or changing doctors, you will need to contact your old doctor in writing to have your medical records transferred.

Ask questions before reading a contract. If the answers do not match the written words, do not sign.

You have the right to read the warranty in advance of purchasing a product.

Consequential damages are things that happen indirectly from an act of the party. Warranties do not cover consequential damages.

If your coffee maker breaks and floods your kitchen, the damaged kitchen is a consequential damage that is not covered under a warranty.

Most warranties only cover repairs if the product is being used properly. A warranty will not cover a TV used to break down a door.

Even though four-wheel-drive vehicles are advertised for off road, their warranties do not cover damages caused by driving off roads.

It is easier to call the Better Business Bureau or a trade association than to fight to recover your money from a bad deal.

Keep the Better Business Bureau's phone number handy. It is easier to call and check on a business than to sue them later.

If you are angry and you are complaining, do not expect the person you are angry at to solve your problem. Most people can only deal with one thing at a time. Your anger will be dealt with, not your problem.

The first one to get angry, loses.

Your date of birth is as valuable as your social security number. All criminal records are kept by date of birth and name.

Creditors worry when they do not hear from their debtors. If you are having a problem, talk to your creditors in advance rather than hiding your head in the sand.

If you are injured on the job, some employers require that you contact a certain doctor or hospital and notify the employer within a certain amount of time.

A notary is only stating that you are the person signing the document. Notaries do not attest to the validity of the document.

Always keep a couple of certified copies of your birth certificate in your safe-deposit box. To obtain copies of your birth certificate, contact the health or records department of the county where you were born.

You should have files in a filing cabinet or someplace safe for documents regarding insurance, your car, home/apartment, loans, products, estate plans, taxes, credit cards, service contracts, repair receipts, applications, divorce papers, passport, driver's license, notices, cancellations, and all other important documents.

Protect your social security number; it is your key to your financial security.

Keep a copy of your passport, credit cards, and driver's license in your safe-deposit box.

Keep two names on your safe-deposit box from two different generations. If one person dies, the survivor can still easily gain entry.

Keep a copy of all of your applications—bank, credit card, insurance, etc. It is always easy to complete a second one from the first and you never know when you may need them.

Buy a filing cabinet, files, and a stapler. Staple your receipt to your warranty and other important information and file it.

Do not have your social security number on your driver's license. With your social security number, a thief can electronically steal you blind.

Criminal Law

A summons is a legal document requiring you to show up at court as a criminal defendant. Summonses are issued for traffic violations and other misdemeanors.

Attorney-client privilege was created so no person, judge or court could be made privy to any conversation between an attorney and his client.

By failing to completely exercise your privilege, you will only hurt yourself.

If you are arrested, do not say anything to anyone.

Never argue with a police officer.

Never resist arrest.

Never give up your right to remain silent, to have an attorney, and to have the attorney present during any questioning.

Never admit anything to the police about your friends. If they threaten you, ask to see a lawyer.

You are innocent until proven guilty, no matter what you hear on television.

You are innocent if the jury says you are innocent no matter what the TV commentator says.

If it is out in the open, you can be arrested for possessing it.

Misdemeanors are criminal actions where the fine is small, less than $1,000.00, and the jail term is minimal – one year or less.

A felony is a criminal offense where you can be incarcerated for one year or more in the state or federal penitentiary system.

If you already knew what a misdemeanor and a felony are, you are in law school or you have seen the inside of a jail.

If you are robbed or assaulted, remember what was said and what the person looked like.

Crying, begging, threatening, screaming, or yelling at a cop is the best way to guarantee you are going to go to jail.

That it is better 100 guilty Persons should escape than that one innocent Person should suffer, is a Maxim that has been long and generally approved.
—Benjamin Franklin

The love of justice in most men is only the fear of themselves suffering by injustice.
—Francois de La Rochefoucauld

Traffic Laws and Tickets

Traffic laws vary from state, city, and county. What you can do in your home county is not a defense to what you did to be pulled over in a different county.

Driving laws vary from state to state; driving habits vary more.

Driving tickets not paid in one state will appear in your state as a warrant for your arrest in your state. You will not be arrested but you probably will not be able to renew your licenses.

With your driver's license and a few dollars, you can get a copy of your driving record. You should check your driving record every few years.

Always wear your seat belt. You can be fined for not wearing your seat belt in most states. You may also die if you do not wear your seat belt.

Do not drink and drive.

Traffic tickets make money for the government.

When you get your prescription filled, ask your doctor if it is OK to drive while taking the prescription.

Driving under the influence of prescription drugs is still illegal.

Know your legal limit to consume alcohol and never exceed it with your car keys in your pocket.

Your attorney can tell you which insurance company handles claims well and treats its policyholders well. Buy your insurance from that company, not the cheapest.

Do not keep your car registration and garage door opener in your car. You have given a thief access and the address to rob your home.

Do not keep your home address on your keys for your home. If a thief finds them, he will have all that is needed to find and enter your home.

Estate Planning

There is no such thing as a free lunch. You have to give up something to get something. To qualify for Medicaid, you have to be broke.

Do not rely on any government to take care of you in your old age.

When having an attorney prepare a will, take the legal names, addresses, and counties of residence of all your relatives and heirs with you.

A power of attorney is as important as a will. You have a greater chance of disability than death.

A durable power of attorney becomes effective when you are unable to take care of yourself or when you are under a disability.

A durable power of attorney allows your agent to handle your affairs when you are disabled or unable to take care of yourself.

Check your will every three years to make sure your desires or the laws have not changed.

A living will is a valuable gift to your doctor and your relatives. It takes the monumental decision off their shoulders.

Trusts are used to avoid paying estate taxes.

Trusts are used to avoid giving money to people.

Keep your burial instructions out of your safe-deposit box. They do no one any good locked away while you are being buried.

Keep your burial instructions at home, with a copy at your mortuary and with a good friend.

Make a will; your children will appreciate it.

Make a will; your employees will appreciate it.

Make a will; your grandchildren will appreciate it.

Make a will; your spouse will appreciate it.

You need a will to make sure the right person becomes the guardian in charge of your kids.

When you move to a new state, you may need to change your will.

You need a will to make sure the right person becomes the conservator of the money for your children. This is not necessarily the same person as the children's guardian.

Powers of attorney must be revoked in writing.

Wills must be physically destroyed to no longer be valid. Rip it up, safely burn it, or tear off the signature line to destroy your will.

If you forgive your debts in a will, the forgiven debt is not income to the recipient of a loan.

Do not use your will as a means to control people. You lose once you die.

Trusts are used to distribute money a certain way after someone dies.

Discuss your burial plans with your spouse, children, and executor — before you die.

Prepare a living will; your doctor will appreciate it.

Be an organ donor and someone will never forget you.

Seriously consider spending your children's inheritance.

Bequeathing a cherished object will remind the recipient of you long after a gift of money has been spent.

Trusts can be great for stopping the IRS and providing money to help children grow up.

Creating a trust will not do you any good unless you transfer your property to the trust, immediately.

Put not Your trust in money, but put your money in trust.
—Oliver Wendell Holmes.

Testamentary means at death. A testamentary trust means one formed at death by a will.

Irrevocable means once formed you cannot change it.

Revocable means the document can be changed at any time.

Inter vivos, or living trust, means one formed during the lifetime of the persons.

An organ donor card is a valuable gift to someone.

If a parent or loved one is physically having trouble paying regular monthly bills, see if you can have the bills automatically withdrawn from their checking account.

Medicare and most medigap insurance policies do not cover the cost of long-term nursing care. If you have significant assets, you may want to investigate this type of policy.

If you are providing more than half of a parent's support, you may want to consider claiming your parent as a deduction.

Death certificates can be located in the county where the person died, usually through the health department.

Paper, Promises and Voice: Contracts

Never sign anything without reading it.

Never sign anything without understanding it.

A lifetime contract should raise questions. There are few things besides eating we want to do for a lifetime.

Do you still want to receive *Teenager* magazine after your kids have graduated from college and left home? Be wary of telephone magazine sales and long-term magazine contracts.

Contracts can be oral; they do not have to be written in most states.

Always read the fine print.

Always understand the fine print.

Any document that is to be filed should be prepared by an attorney.

A release is a document that prevents you from suing if you are injured. Releases do work.

Prepare and sign a buy/sell agreement; your business associates will appreciate it.

Never sign any agreement unless it says it can be canceled without penalty until your attorney has read and approved it.

Any deadline is extendible if a sale is involved.

Service contracts usually do not start until after the warranty period has ended.

Make sure you get to see and read a service contract before you purchase it. It may be worthless paper.

Always find out who stands behind the service contact. If it is offered by your local store, they may go out of business without the reserves to continue funding your contract.

When buying a service contract, check the deductible amount and the exclusions. If the exclusions section is longer then the rest of the contract be wary.

Always understand how a service contract works. Can you take it back to the store or do you have to send it to the other side of the world?

Sometimes you can purchase a service contract later, before your warranty ends. This will give you the opportunity to decide if you need a service contract.

If you co-sign a loan, you are promising to pay the loan when your lover leaves town. Make sure you have enough money to pay the loan and you really love that person.

Anyone who asks you for money or a loan, or to co-sign a loan in a new relationship, intends to live off you but probably not with you.

Some studies show that 3 out of 4 co-signed loans are paid by the co-signer.

When you co-sign a loan, the information is placed on your credit record just as if you had signed the loan as borrower.

You do not always have the right to be notified when your friend skips town on the loan you co-signed. Get this promise in writing from the lender so you are prepared when the knock comes on the door.

If you do not understand the cancellation procedures in a contract, do not sign the contract. You probably cannot cancel the contract.

Non-refundable means you will not get your money back, no matter what.

Sold "as is" means what you see is what you get—no warranty, no return and no repair, no matter what you were told.

Notices and cancellations need to be in writing. Always keep a copy of any notice or cancellation.

Any deadline is extendible.

Trying to learn the Declaration of Independence by having someone read it to you is difficult. Do not expect your attorney to answer contract questions by you reading the contract over the phone.

Paraphrasing a contract to a lawyer will cost you money. Millions of dollars can ride on the difference between “and” and “or.”

When signing any contract, look for the language that protects the other guy and read it.

Always understand your contracts. Most contracts have a series of procedures or appeals you must undertake before you can sue for breach of contract.

When purchasing extended service agreements, make sure the start date is the date you purchase the item. Many will start 30 days later, after all the parts have malfunctioned and you have replaced them at your cost.

Anytime someone attempts to scratch out parts of a typeset contract to change something, be wary. Lawyers wrote the typesetting. Who is making the change?

An extended service agreement with a $100.00 deductible and a thirty-day waiting period is worthless.

Real Estate and Homes

Title companies are insurance companies. They pay claims the same way, reluctantly.

Buying real property from the owner without a bank requires legal help.

Buying or selling real property without a realtor should be done with the assistance of an attorney.

Buying a house is not an excuse that can be used to get you out of an apartment lease.

It is not easy to live with neighbors you are having a dispute with after you have called a police officer about them. Remember that when you are contemplating reporting your neighbor to the police.

Unless you sign a contract for a realtor to represent you, the realtor always represents the seller.

Never buy real estate unless you have stood on it a couple of times. Pictures lie, and so do salespersons.

Salespersons selling land for investment purposes intend to retire on your money.

If you are shopping for a mortgage locking in a rate, remember that "lock-in's" need to be in writing and come from the loan underwriter, not the loan salesman.

A loan commitment is a promise to make you a loan. That is different from a locked-in loan rate.

Realtors are not lawyers. When you make a $100,000.00 purchase, spend $1000.00 to make sure it is done right.

Understand your real estate title policy exclusions. Those are items the title company is not going to cover.

Find out from a bank how much house you can buy; then go shopping for a home.

A bottle of wine, sleeping bags, and candles are a good way to spend a night in a home you are thinking about buying. You will learn about your lover, yourself, your house, and your neighbors.

Drive to and from your new house or apartment during rush hour.

When financing a home with an adjustable rate mortgage, make sure you can afford the mortgage at the maximum increase allowed over the next three years.

If you buy a house in a homeowners' association or a condominium, you are buying ownership with all the other people in the association.

Condominium ownership or housing communities provide an additional group of people to tell you how to run your home.

If you are offered free or cheap airfare to go look at property, the property is probably overpriced. Somehow that airfare must be paid.

If a piece of real estate is subject to the Federal Full Disclosure Act, you have seven days to cancel the purchase without penalty and get your money back.

If you have purchased a time-share, a new scam comes from time-share re-sellers. For a large fee, they will re-sell your time-share to someone on their large list of interested buyers.

The actual market for reselling a time-share is poor. Over the last 20 years, only 3.3% of time-shares have actually sold.

Insurance

Check with your insurance company before you move to determine what type of coverage you will have for your possessions during the move.

Based on what insurance you have and your deductibles, you may need to buy additional insurance from your mover.

"No-fault" insurance means your insurance company pays your bills.

If you live in a "no-fault" state, you need to make sure you and your insurance company get along.

Understand the risk and the amount of money at risk when evaluating insurance.

Ask your insurance agent how often the average claim of a certain type occurs. If raising your deductible will save you enough money to pay the deductible difference in that amount of time, it is worthwhile to take the higher deductible.

When you lease a car, your auto insurance must cover the difference between the contract lease value and the car value if you total the car. If your insurance company will not pay the difference, you will.

Your homeowner's insurance does not cover floods. Only flood insurance, a separate and distinct policy, covers floods. Flood insurance is sold by the federal government.

Your attorney can tell you which insurance company handles claims well and treats its policyholders well. Buy your insurance from that company, not the cheapest.

Photo inventory your home and possessions every year. In the event your home is destroyed, it provides valuable proof of possession and value

When you have a claim for damaged property, you will be required to list what you lost and what its value is. For even a small house, this is impossible unless you have prepared your list or photos in advance.

Your homeowner's or apartment insurance policy provides only limited coverage for your possessions not on your property. Make sure you have enough insurance if you have a storage unit.

Your flooded kitchen should be covered under your homeowner's policy.

Insurance premiums are cheap compared to the amount of money you may receive in a claim.

Your apartment insurance should protect you from your landlord if the apartment is destroyed while you are renting it.

Homeowner's, condominium, and tenant insurance are all different. Make sure you have the right policy for where you are living.

If you are renting a condominium, you may need a condominium insurance policy, rather than a tenant insurance policy.

If you are denied a claim from an insurance company, resubmit the claim later. A different person may see the claim differently and pay it.

Most drivers file auto insurance claims once every 10 years.

Business and the Law

Business plans are necessary to start a business. They provide a blueprint for preparing to open your doors and a base to rely on when something goes wrong.

If you want to make bad points with someone, yell at his staff or receptionists for the problems their boss created.

Copyright law is just like grade school. You cannot hand in a book report you copied word for word from the encyclopedia and call it your own.

You need a "permit" to do anything.

A good CPA is the first person you should hire when starting a business.

A good lawyer is second.

Your CPA can usually refer you to a good lawyer.

Join the Better Business Bureau; it will give you a leg up on a complaint.

When you join the Better Business Bureau, learn and follow their rules.

Join your trade associations and attend their conventions. You can turn competitors into friends while in a faraway location having fun.

By attending conferences and trade shows, you learn the latest and newest industry information. Keeping up with the industry is important for competition and keeping litigation at bay.

Your CPA is the best friend of a businessperson trying to get a loan.

Find a banker, not a bank. Get to know your banker. Establish a relationship with him.

Make your bank deposits yourself. Stay in touch with your bankers. Some banks still loan based on your reputation rather than a computer program.

Forming a corporation is easy; keeping it going properly is a little harder. Just remember to have a minimum of five meetings a year: four quarterly board meetings and one yearly shareholders' meeting.

Do not use a corporate check to pay for personal items. That is the easiest way to lose your corporation.

Partnerships are like marriages—and just as hard to dissolve.

It is easier to deal with an angry customer than a calm lawyer.

Negotiating the deal correctly the first time is always cheaper than suing or negotiating the second time.

Ask questions during the negotiations. It is cheaper to arrange solutions to possible problems than it is to measure damages.

Landlords and Rental Agreements

A lease is a contract where you agree to pay rent for the period of time specified on the lease, no matter what.

Just because someone else caused your problem does not mean you can avoid your contractual obligations, like the rent.

Leases are legal contracts.

Do not move into a new apartment until all of the promises made by the landlord have been met. Once you become a tenant, you lose any bargaining power.

To receive your security deposit back after you vacate an apartment, you must leave the apartment as clean as you found it and provide the landlord with an address to send the deposit.

Photograph your apartment before you move in, especially broken or damaged walls or rooms. Have the film developed immediately so the date will show when the photos were taken. A photo is good evidence of the preexisting damages when you leave.

Photograph an apartment after you have moved out to prove the cleanliness and undamaged conditions. Develop the film when you need it.

Ask to see the apartment you will be renting, not just the model they are showing.

Spend one night in your future apartment before you sign a lease. A sleeping bag and good book will help you learn about neighbors, noise, and inconvenience.

You may not own much, but tenant's insurance will protect you if your pet bites someone.

If you are preparing to sign a lease with a lover, make sure the relationship will last the term of the lease. Breaking up is not an excuse to get out of a lease.

You are responsible for your apartment until your landlord accepts responsibility for it. Just because you are not living there does not mean you are not liable for it.

Family Matters

If you are leaving your children with family or friends for a period of time, leave them with a child care authorization so they can take your kid to a doctor or hospital without problems.

If you are leaving for an extended period of time, contact your children's school and provide them with a copy of the child care authorization and child care instructions so they will allow your children to be picked up by whoever is taking care of them.

Credit Cards

If you dispute a charge on your credit card, you can withhold payment. However, you must pay the interest charge on the disputed amount.

If you are divorced without a credit card in your name, you can apply for a credit card in your name based on your ex-spouse's credit history.

When you stay at a hotel or motel and use a credit card, the hotel immediately reserves the entire cost of the stay plus estimated extras on your card. Sometimes this can be several times the amount you would expect.

Car rental agencies block amounts from your credit card also.

If your credit card is stolen, report it missing immediately. You can only be charged a maximum of $50.00 for purchases made by a thief until you report the card.

After you report a credit card stolen, you cannot be charged for any purchases made by the thief.

If your ATM card is stolen, you must report it to your bank within two days. If you do so, you can only lose up to $50.00.

If you fail to report your ATM card stolen within two days, you can lose up to $500.00.

Mistakes on credit cards can be corrected if you notify them in writing and within the time limit allowed, sixty days.

Credit card companies then have 30 days to respond to your complaint and must resolve the complaint within 90 days.

Banks are safer than ATMs.

It is easier to get your money back if you pay with a credit card.

Most combinations, PIN codes, or access codes are numbers you easily remember—birth date, social security number, or phone number. Thieves know this also.

Always examine replacement credit cards. Make sure the name and numbers are the same and sign the cards immediately.

Insurance

Most health, life, and disability insurance companies report your health information to the Medical Information Bureau. Like a credit bureau, the Medical Information Bureau keeps track of your health information and is used by insurance companies to deny claims on policies.

Look at filing health insurance claims as making money. Any claims you are entitled to and have not been reimbursed for will pay you that amount for the hour it will take to complete the claim form.

Try not to burn a bridge when you leave a job. You never know when you may need a reference or need to go back.

If you are being terminated from your job, don't be afraid to ask for the world. What are they going to do—fire you?

If you are injured on the job, some employers require that you contact a certain doctor or hospital and notify the employer within a certain amount of time.

Treat your employees the way you want to be treated if you want them to stay.

A prostitute is cheaper than a sexual harassment lawsuit.

Learn and understand the difference between a good employee who makes a mistake and a bad employee.

The employer generally gets the employees he deserves.
—Walter Gilbey

Buying a Car and Not Paying with Blood

Gross capitalization cost is what you are paying for the car when you lease it. If the gross capitalization cost is more than the sticker price or the price on the car, you are being ripped off.

If you are buying a car with a friend, make sure the friendship will last or have a way to recover the car if it doesn't.

If you are buying a car with a friend, make sure the friendship will last the length of the loan. You will have to cover the car payment if your friend doesn't.

Many car dealers will have you sign a disclosure form when you purchase a car that states you will pay a different interest rate if you do not get financed the first time. If you sign that disclosure, you will end up paying the higher interest rate if the dealer can find a reason.

Car dealers require you to sign a lot of paperwork when you buy a car.

Most car dealers make you sign one contract waiving all of your rights and another contract acknowledging the fact you waived your rights.

When you walk onto a car dealer's lot, ask to see the paperwork you will sign to buy a car first. Start reading the documents then. It will take a long while to understand what you are signing.

Go to a bank and get your loan approved before you go buy a car.

Automobile leases always look good going in and can hurt coming out.

Car dealers make money on the car loans they sell.

Even though a car dealer is having you fill out the loan paperwork, he is not going to be handling your loan.

Car dealers use a bait and switch tactic in financing car deals. You buy the car at one finance rate and leave the lot. After you have had the car for awhile you are turned down on the loan and you must come back to sign new documents. You cannot turn the car back in because the documents say if you do you have rented the car at a ridiculous rental rate per mile and/or per day.

When buying an automobile, make sure you understand the mileage charge and the rental charge if your financing does not go through. Once you sign on the dotted line and leave the lot your home mortgage may be cheaper than what you'll pay for the car.

Finances

Always meet the people from whom you are borrowing money.

Life insurance is not an investment.

Several government or private agencies insure banks and stock-brokers. However, the insurance does not pay immediately. Your money can be tied up for months while things are sorted out.

Life and the Law

There is no such thing as a free lunch, unless dad is still buying.

The younger you are the more important the Bill of Rights.

Always anticipate the unexpected.

Laws vary from state to state.

When you turn 18, get a passport. It is easy to do and cheap when you do not need it.

A passport is a great temporary replacement for an ID to cash checks and enter adult establishments.

Always carry your divorce decree or name change documents with your passport until you get your passport changed.

If you want to serve on a board, get a copy of *Robert's Rules of Order*. Learn them and use them to move things along.

Legally plan for all contingencies—death, divorce, bankruptcy — no matter how well things are going.

Every other birthday, check your passport expiration date.

Every birthday, check your driver's license.

Buy your car on your birthday; it will make it easy to renew your license plates. It makes a great birthday present.

Your credit report is valuable, check it yearly.

It is sad, but you will have more need for copies of your divorce decree than you will your marriage license.

Marriage licenses are kept in the records department in the state and county where the marriage license was issued, not necessarily where the marriage was performed.

The first amendment to the Constitution guarantees the right to free speech.

Whenever you hear something you do not like or an opinion different from your own, smile. The exercise of freedom of speech guarantees you the right to not like what you hear and to speak your opinion in opposition.

The XVI amendment to the United States Constitution is rarely quoted. If you want to impress people, use it as a threat. It allows the government to collect taxes.

Know your legislators, and let them know you know them.

If your organ donor card is on the back of your driver's license, do not forget to sign the card each time you get a new license.

Children are not property. You should not hold your children hostage in a divorce. You should also not allow your children to hold you hostage in a divorce.

If you cannot handle getting a pre-nuptial agreement, how are you going to handle being married?

Always do right; this will gratify some people and astonish the rest.
—Mark Twain

People demand freedom of speech to make up for the freedom of thought which they avoid.
—Sören Kierkegaard

Freedom rings where opinions clash.
—Adlai E. Stevenson

Children are innocent and love justice, while most adults are wicked and prefer mercy.
—Gilbert K. Chesterton

The Bill of Rights should be read once a year by everyone. As you age, they become clearer.

Children are not property.

There is no such thing as a free lunch unless you live at home or have a key to your parents' house.

When you finally do feel as if you can throw documents away, recycle them.

You need to keep most important documents for a minimum of seven years.

It is always cheaper and easier to do something right the first time than to correct the mistakes.

The statute of limitations for murder and failing to file a federal tax return is the same — forever.

When a man tells you that he got rich through hard work, ask him: "whose?"
—Don Marquis

An organ donor card is a valuable gift to someone.

Every once in awhile read the Declaration of Independence. It has a different meaning once you graduate from civics class.

About the Author

Jim Moss is a trial attorney licensed to practice law in Colorado and Ohio as well as the Colorado Federal Courts and the Tenth Circuit court of Appeals. He is a sole practitioner specializing in insurance defense work, business litigation. He handles consumer problems when a great one appears or the underdog is in the corner.

When not practicing law, he speaks and consults with businesses on ways to avoid lawsuits. His ideas on lawsuit prevention have been used nationwide to stop injured parties before ever going to lawyers or trial. These simple ideas have proved extremely effective in eliminating lawsuits with minimal cost and some time and concern. Most lawsuits are an emotional issue not a monetary issue and Mr. Moss' ideas on dealing with those issues have proven extremely effective. His ideas have been used on litigation, personal injury actions, breach of contract and wrongful death cases.

Mr. Moss can be reached at 303-980-5353, fax 303-989-2316, 12340 W. Alameda Pkwy., Lakewood, Colorado

NEW ADVISOR SERIES

The Medical Advisor

The Medical Advisor: 500 maxims and tips for patients and providers By Thomas Meade M.D.

Physicians and patients will understand one another better with the Medical Advisor. More than eighteen years of professional health care experience at all levels of the provider spectrum, lace this compact but potent gift book. Give it to your nurse, your doctor or a medical student you know. Understand your doctor better and enjoy a healthy relationship.
Sections for physicians, patients, surgeons, physicians in training, nurses, physician assistants, sport medicine providers, managed care providers, physical therapy providers, law, medicine and more.

About the author

Thomas D Meade M.D. is a Clinical Assistant Professor of Orthopedic Surgery at The Pennsylvania State University, Hershey Medical Center, Attending Orthopedic Surgeon at Lehigh Valley Hospital/Regional Trauma Center, Medical Director of Allentown Sports Medicine and Human Performance Center, Team Physician for Muhlenberg College and five local high schools.

Typical comments include:

As a physician, remember physicians die young and have a high divorce rate

. . . There's a lesson here somewhere.

As a physician, you should be a patient at least once a year.

As a surgeon, use two criteria: "Would I have the operation?" and "Would I have the operation if money was not involved?"

$9.95 paperback • 13.50 Canada

4 x 7 • 160 pages • ISBN 1-57034-049-8